1925) called his spiritual philosophy 'anthroposophy', meaning 'wisdom of the human being'. As a highly developed seer, he based his work on direct knowledge and perception of spiritual dimensions. He initiated a modern and universal 'science of spirit', accessible to anyone willing to exercise clear and unprejudiced thinking.

From his spiritual investigations Steiner provided suggestions for the renewal of many activities, including education (both general and special), agriculture, medicine, economics, architecture, science, philosophy, religion and the arts. Today there are thousands of schools, clinics, farms and other organizations involved in practical work based on his principles. His many published works feature his research into the spiritual nature of the human being, the evolution of the world and humanity, and methods of personal development. Steiner wrote some 30 books and delivered over 6000 lectures across Europe. In 1924 he founded the General Anthroposophical Society, which today has branches throughout the world.

HOW TO CURE NERVOUSNESS

RUDOLF STEINER

Sophia Books

Sophia Books
An imprint of Rudolf Steiner Press
Hillside House, The Square
Forest Row RH18 5ES

www.rudolfsteinerpress.com

Published by Rudolf Steiner Press 2008

First published in a translation by R.M. Querido and
G. Church by Anthroposophic Press in 1978

This translation revised by Matthew Barton
© Rudolf Steiner Press 2008

Originally published in German as part of the volume entitled
*Erfahungen des Übersinnlichen, Die drei Wege der Seele zu
Christus* (volume 143 in the *Rudolf Steiner Gesamtausgabe* or
Collected Works) by Rudolf Steiner Verlag, Dornach. This
authorized translation is published by permission of the Rudolf
Steiner Nachlassverwaltung, Dornach

A catalogue record for this book is available from the British
Library

ISBN 978 185584 208 3

Cover by Andrew Morgan
Typeset by DP Photosetting, Neath, West Glamorgan
Printed and bound in Great Britain by Cromwell Press Limited,
Trowbridge, Wiltshire

Contents

Today let us try to enlarge the picture we are already familiar with. Some of you may find what I have to say useful, since it leads to a more precise idea of the nature of the human being and his relationship with the world.

Anthroposophists[1] often encounter objections to spiritual science. Both academics and lay people criticize the fourfold division of the human being into physical body, etheric body, astral body and ego or 'I'.[2] These sceptics often say that even if some people may perceive these things by developing hidden soul forces, others—who do not—have no need to concern themselves with such ideas. But let me stress that if one is attentive to life, it will itself confirm what spiritual science has to say. Furthermore, the teachings of anthroposophy can prove

1

extremely useful in everyday life. This useful-ness, not of a merely utilitarian kind, but use-fulness in the finest sense, gradually but convincingly comes to inform the outlook even of people who do not particularly desire to engage with clairvoyant perception.

Now let's consider nervousness, a common and widespread complaint with all sorts of symptoms. It hardly seems surprising to hear that we are all affected by it in some way, as is readily understood if we consider the con-temporary social conditions which exacerbate it.

Nervousness manifests in various ways—most obviously perhaps where someone's thoughts jump about all over the place, so that he's unable to hold a single idea in his head let alone pursue a train of thought to its conclusion. This kind of continual, mental fidgeting or hastiness of the soul is the most common form of nervousness.

Another is when people do not know what to do with themselves and are unable to take a clear initiative. When called upon to make a decision they are at a loss to know what to do. This condition can lead to more severe symptoms, perhaps ultimately manifesting in various forms of psychosomatic disorder that simulate organic illnesses. Supposed gastric disorders are an example of this, whose real cause is relatively trivial and can be summarized as nervousness. One might mention many other conditions—we are all familiar with them, either because we suffer from them ourselves or because others in our surroundings do—such as the 'political alcoholism' apparent in important events of public life. This expression was coined to describe the sort of nervous frenzy with which politicians in Europe have been conducting themselves in recent months; a kind of behaviour that you only otherwise see in someone on the edge of alcoholism. Here one not only observes the presence of nervousness but also its unpleasant and prevalent effects.

We can be sure there will be no improvement

in these symptoms in the near future. They are only likely to get worse, and prospects for the future are not good if people remain as they are at present. Many harmful factors strongly affect our lives, passing like an epidemic from one person to another, and thus also infecting those who are basically healthy but just a little weak or susceptible.

It is extremely harmful for our times that many people who hold high and responsible positions in public life have been compelled to study as people do nowadays. Whole branches of learning are taught in a way that prevents students, throughout the entire university year, from spending time and energy on really thinking through and absorbing what their professors teach them. As a result, when exams come round they have to 'cram' for them. This cramming, though, has dire effects, also on school pupils to some extent, because it allows the soul no real means to properly connect with the subject matter. No wonder that students are often keen to forget as quickly as possible what they have just had to learn! Thus the core of the human soul is only very tenuously connected with what has to be learned.

What impact do these educational methods have? In some respects, no doubt, people are getting the training they need to engage in public life. But the schooling they receive means that they do not unite inwardly with their work. They feel emotionally remote from what their heads are doing. Now there is nothing worse than to feel remote in your heart from the things you have to do with your head. Not only is this repugnant to sensitive people but it also has a very adverse effect on the strength of the etheric body. If, in the core of his soul, a person has only a tenuous interest in his professional pursuits, this gradually weakens his etheric body. The very opposite effect comes about, however, when people adopt anthroposophy in a healthy way. More than just learning that we consist of physical body, etheric body, astral body and 'I', such a person will also develop in a way that enables these aspects to unfold strongly and harmoniously in him.

Even a simple experiment, if repeated diligently, can often work wonders. Forgive me if I now discuss what may seem small and trivial observations. In fact they can be of great significance for human life. Take slight forgetfulness, for example—something fairly widespread and a nuisance. Anthroposophy tells us in fact that it is harmful to health, and that, strange as it may seem, many disorders bordering on severe illness could be avoided if people managed to be less forgetful. Now you may say, 'Well that's just how people are—nothing to be done about it.' No one is exempt—everyone is forgetful to some degree. Just think of the numerous instances when people forget where they left something. One person keeps losing his pencil, another cannot find his cufflinks, etc.—all these incidents seem trivial, but they occur pretty frequently in daily life.

There is actually a good exercise for gradually curing such forgetfulness. Suppose that a woman repeatedly forgets in the morning where she put her brooch when she took it off the night before. You might think that the best cure for such forgetfulness would be for her to remember to put it in the same place each time. But there is a far more effective means of remembering where it is. Of course this doesn't work for all objects, but in this case the woman should say to herself: 'I will place my brooch somewhere different each night, but as I do so I will retain in my mind the thought that I have put it in this particular place. I will form a clear picture in my mind of its precise surroundings.' Let's imagine we place a safety pin on the edge of a table, on its corner, and as we do so form a clear image of the right-angle of the table, with the safety pin positioned between the table's two edges. Then we leave it there confidently. If I only do this once it probably won't work, but if I make a habit of it, my forgetfulness will gradually improve.

This exercise works because we form a very specific thought—that I'm placing the safety pin in a particular place and surroundings. By doing this I consciously connect my ego or 'I' with the action I take, and also form a clear picture. Picturing what I do as I think about it, connecting my 'I', the spiritual core of my being, with a pictorial image, sharpens the memory. Such an exercise can help us become less forgetful.

This kind of exercise, however, can also achieve a great deal more. When it becomes a habit to retain such thoughts as we put things down, this increasingly strengthens the etheric body—which as we know from anthroposophy underpins memory in a certain sense. If we do something that strengthens our powers of memory, it is easy to understand that this is also of use to our etheric or life body. But now assume that you have advised someone to practise this exercise not because he is forgetful but because he is nervous. It will prove an excellent cure that not only improves his memory but also strengthens his etheric body—his nervous tendencies will gradually disappear. In such cases life itself shows the correctness of what spiritual science teaches. If we relate to the etheric body in the right way then it shows us itself how it acquires these enhanced forces, and that what we say about it is true.

Here is another example that might also appear trivial at first glance, but is actually extraordinarily important. You know that the physical and etheric bodies directly adjoin and connect with each other. Now anyone with healthy sensitivity will feel compassion for clerical workers and others whose professions require a great deal of writing. You may have noticed the following fairly widespread phenomenon: strange motions such people sometimes make in the air when about to write. Before they begin to write the letter B for instance, they first make a few motions in the air and then bring the pen to bear on the paper. In some cases these movements are less discernible—the person may only give a slight jerk before he starts to write, repeating this before every upstroke and downstroke. You can see this jerkiness in the writing itself.

Spiritual science can easily give insight into this condition. In a healthy human being the etheric body, guided by the astral body, must always have the capacity to fully penetrate the physical body, so that the physical body acts as the etheric body's servant in all its movements. But when, unguided by the astral body, the physical body executes movements of its own, over and above what the soul, the astral body, desires or intends, this is symptomatic of an unhealthy condition. These jerks show that the etheric has become subservient to the physical body, and that the weak etheric body can no longer fully guide and direct the physical. Clairvoyant perception can see that every form of cramp or convulsion is based on such a relationship between the physical and etheric bodies, in which the physical body dominates and makes motions of its own. In a healthy person, by contrast, all movements are subordinate to the will of the astral body working through the etheric.

Once again, as long as the condition has not become too extreme, there is a way to help someone with these symptoms by considering the supersensible facts. In this case we must recognize the existence and mode of action of the etheric body, and try to enhance it. Imagine someone so worn down that his fingers start shaking and jerking whenever he tries to write. Of course, it would be good to tell him to write less and take a good holiday; but this is only half a solution. Better still is to suggest that he also try to acquire a different form of handwriting. Tell him to stop writing automatically and to try paying conscious attention to the way he forms his letters. Fifteen minutes a day is enough— strenuous efforts are not needed. Tell him to try shaping his handwriting differently, and to develop the habit of drawing the letters. For instance, instead of writing the letter F in the normal way, he can try to give it a narrower, more upright form. The point of this is that when someone consciously changes his handwriting he is forced to fully attend to what he is doing and connect the inmost core of his being with it.

If spiritual science were to become more widespread, when such a person came back from holiday having acquired a different form of handwriting, his manager wouldn't upbraid him for this but would see it is as a substantial remedy. Everything which connects the inmost core of our being with what we do strengthens our etheric or life body, so that we become healthier.

It wouldn't be a bad idea to introduce such exercises systematically into the classroom, to strengthen the etheric body even during childhood. But even though anthroposophy can give this kind of educational advice, it will doubtless be a long time before leading educators think it anything other than foolish. Nevertheless, suppose that children were first taught a particular form of handwriting, and then, after a few years were expected to learn an entirely different way of forming their script. The change, and the conscious attention involved in this, would lead to a remarkable strengthening of the etheric body, and some of the nervous conditions we see today would never arise.

So you see, things can be done to strengthen the etheric body. This is immensely important because nowadays it is precisely the weakness of the etheric body that leads to many unhealthy conditions. One can even say—and this really isn't going too far—that certain forms of illness and disorder, rooted in causes that fail to respond to treatment, would take a quite different course if the etheric body were stronger. Weakened etheric bodies really are a typical characteristic of modern human beings.

What I have suggested here is a definite way

of working on the etheric body. By practising these exercises a real force can be brought to bear on the etheric body, which could not be brought to bear if the existence of this body is denied. When the effects of such actions become apparent, though, the results themselves demonstrate that the etheric body exists. Life itself everywhere confirms the insights of anthroposophy.

The etheric body can also be strengthened by practising another exercise, in this case one to improve memory. In all forms of disorder in which nervousness plays a part one should take up such suggestions. Thinking through events, not just in the sequence they occurred but also in reverse—that is, by starting at the end of an event and thinking back through it to the beginning—helps enormously to strengthen the etheric body. Historical events, for instance, which are usually learned in chronological sequence, can be traced in reverse. Or you can work backwards through a play or story from its end to its beginning. When done conscientiously, such exercises are highly effective for consolidating and strengthening the etheric body.

If you reflect on this it soon becomes clear that people do not do the things that would help enhance the etheric body. The hectic, daily bustle of modern life does not give them a chance to access the inner quiet needed for such exercises. In the evening, after their day's work, they are usually too tired to bother with these things. If spiritual science began to permeate their hearts and minds, however, people would start to see that many things accomplished in a frantic way every day would become redundant; and they would find time to practise such exercises. They would also become aware of the potentially positive results of placing emphasis on such things in school curricula.

Let me mention another little exercise here. If not cultivated from early youth it may not be quite so useful in later life. But it is still helpful to practise it later on. This is to look carefully at whatever we do, whether or not it has any lasting importance. This is comparatively easy when writing, and if many people really looked carefully at each letter, one by one, allowing the gaze to pass again over what has been written, they would, I am sure, soon improve their dire handwriting.

Yet another exercise involves a person observing himself closely—the way he walks, moves his head, laughs, etc. In short, he should try to form a clear image of his own movements and gestures. Few people actually know, for instance, what they look like when they're walking. Though it is good to undertake this as an experiment it should not be prolonged as it would quickly lead to vanity. Quite apart from the fact that the exercise can correct undesirable habits, it also tends to consolidate the etheric body, and enhance the astral body's mastery over the etheric body. When someone cultivates awareness of his gestures and involuntary actions, when he forms a conception of his actions, the astral is given ever-increasing control over the etheric. People are actually less and less able nowadays to voluntarily suppress in themselves habitual actions, or to do things differently.

To be able to do quite differently the things we do habitually is an excellent accomplishment. Nowadays people only alter their handwriting for illegal purposes. I am not proposing to train forgers when I suggest that changing one's handwriting will help to consolidate the etheric body. The essential thing here is the benefit gained from occasionally altering the habitual ways in which we do things, rather than always being compelled to do something in one way only. This does not mean that we need to be fanatical, say, about using our right and left hands interchangeably. But if someone can occasionally do with his left hand what he otherwise usually does with the right, he will strengthen the astral body's control over his etheric body. Strengthening people in ways that are based on the insights of spiritual science is something that our culture needs.

What we can call the cultivation of the will is also most important. I have already mentioned that nervousness often expresses itself in the fact that people do not know how to do what they really want, or feel they ought to want. They are scared of carrying out their intentions, and sit on the fence instead. We can regard this as a weakness of will due to the ego's insufficient control over the astral body initially. In the case of such weakness of will, the ego's mastery of the astral body is always deficient. People do not quite know what they want; and if they do, they fail to act on it. Still others are unable to really want what they wish they wanted.

In fact there is a simple means to strengthen the will, and it is this: to suppress wishes that are doubtless present—provided of course that it does no harm to leave a wish unfulfilled, and that this is entirely possible in a particular instance. Just examine your own life and you will find countless desires it would no doubt be pleasant to satisfy, but equally possible to leave unsatisfied. Fulfilling them would give you pleasure, but you can manage perfectly well without; and failure to fulfil them will not harm anyone else either or be a dereliction of duty. If you set out to examine yourself systematically in this way, every act of restraint will signify additional strength of will—that is, strength of the ego over the astral body. If we undertake this process in later life it is possible to make good much that was neglected in our earlier education.

Let me stress that it is not easy to apply what has just been described when educating children. For example, if a father refuses to fulfil a wish of his son that he could fulfil, he is likely to arouse the boy's antipathy. Arousing antipathy in this way, you could say, means that refusing to fulfil a child's wish is a poor educational principle. So what can we do? The answer is very simple.

Rather than denying the child, someone with a child or pupil in his care can deny *himself* wishes in a way that allows the child to become aware of this self-restraint. There is a strong imitative impulse at work in the child, especially during the first seven years (but later too as after-effect), and you will soon see that he follows the example of adults around him and becomes able to deny himself wishes. What this achieves is of untold importance. When interest in anthroposophy directs our thoughts in the right way then spiritual science grows in us beyond theory to a wisdom of life that sustains us and enables us to progress.

In two recent lectures I proposed a very important means of strengthening the ego's control over the astral body.[3] There I discussed the importance of being flexible enough to consider what is said not only for but also against an assertion—in other words to see both sides of a problem. Generally people see only one side, but there is really no problem in life for which a one-sided view is adequate. There are always pros and cons. It would be good for us to grow accustomed to always considering not just the pros *or* cons but pros *and* cons of any situation. In the actions we take, too, it is good to be aware of why it would have been better not to do them in certain circumstances; or if it is better that we take these actions, we can still be aware that there are reasons against them.

Human vanity and egotism often mean that we fail to consider the reasons for not doing what we do. In fact, people's desire just to be 'good' often persuades them that they simply need to do what so many favourable reasons seem to suggest is right and disregard the things which so many reasons seem to discount. But we have to realize the uncomfortable fact that many possible objections exist to practically everything we do. People are not nearly as good as they think—and I say this because it is enormously important in life. This is such a general truth as to be of little use—but it can come to be an effective truth if, in everything we do because life demands it, we also consider why we might leave it undone.

Let me give an example to show the practical results that can be achieved by such means. You have probably encountered people so weak-willed that they would prefer never to have to make a decision for themselves. They would like it best if someone else made their decisions for them, leaving them just to carry out what has been decided. Trying to avoid responsibility, they prefer to sit around asking what they should do rather than finding reasons to act. What I am now going to say must also be regarded as having many cons as well as pros. Imagine that a weak-willed person like this is influenced by two others, one of whom says 'Do this' and the other who says 'Don't'. The one whose will exerts the stronger influence on the weak-willed person will prevail. What sort of phenomenon do we have here? It may seem of little importance but is in fact highly significant.

If there are two people, one of whom says 'yes' and the other 'no', and I carry out the first person's 'yes', then his will works on in me, his strength of will has prevailed and has led to my action. His strength of will has prevailed in me over the other person. In other words, another person's strength has triumphed in me.

In contrast to this, however, suppose that I stand alone and, quite independently, face in my own heart the need to make a 'yes' or 'no' decision. Then having answered 'yes', with no one else influencing me, imagine that I go out and do whatever must be done. This 'yes' will have released a strong force, but now within me myself. The effect the other had on me previously I have now created in my own soul. By facing yourself with a conscious choice between two alternatives, you allow strength to prevail over weakness simply by the way in which you make your decision. This is hugely important because it allows the ego's control over the astral body to be strengthened enormously. To really earnestly reflect on the pros and cons in each instance, whenever you can, is not something that should be regarded as a nuisance. Try to practise this and you will find that it greatly helps to strengthen your will.

But this kind of situation also has its darker aspect. Instead of strengthening your will you will only weaken it if, instead of taking an action governed by what speaks in favour of one course rather than another, you neglect to do anything. It will seem as if you have taken the 'no' decision, but in reality you will just have been lax and lazy. If you feel slack and weary it is better not to try to make any choice until you are inwardly strong and know that you will be able to follow through whatever decision is suggested by the pros and cons you weigh up in your mind. It is clear that such choices must be weighed up at the right time.

We also strengthen control of the ego over the astral body when our souls in a certain sense dismiss all that erects a barrier between us and the surrounding world. The anthroposophist should not feel any need to suppress justified criticism if it is objective. It would be weakness to advocate the bad rather than the good for—supposedly—purely spiritual-scientific reasons, and there is absolutely no need to do this. But we must learn to distinguish between something that can be objectively criticized and something at which we take affront, which we find exasperating, simply because of the way it affects us personally. The more we emancipate our judgement, say of our fellow human beings, from what personally affects us, the better it is for strengthening the ego's mastery over the astral body. Thus, not in order to pride ourselves on not criticizing others but to strengthen the ego, it is good to practise the self-denial involved in not necessarily regarding as bad the things in our fellow human beings which may affect us badly. Particularly where other human beings are concerned, we should try only to make negative judgements where we ourselves are not involved. This is easy to say in theory, but really difficult to practise. If someone has lied to you, for instance, rather than going to tell others what he has done, you can try to restrain your feelings of antipathy. Try to observe the way in which he acts and speaks day by day, and let this, rather than what he has done to you, form the basis for judgement. If someone says one thing one day, and another thing on a different day, we just need to compare the two, and we will find a quite different basis for our judgement than if we merely focus on his conduct in one instance.

In this way you allow things to speak for themselves, trying to understand people by the way their different actions relate to each other, rather than judging them on the basis of one particular action. You will find that even in the case of someone widely considered to be a scoundrel there is much that doesn't quite fit this picture, that even contradicts and contrasts with what he himself says or does. You need to disregard your personal relationship with him in order to view him objectively and come to any kind of judgement—if indeed this is really necessary.

In fact, to strengthen the ego it is a good idea to reflect that in all cases we can easily refrain from many of the judgements we utter. To allow just a tenth of them entry to our souls would be more than enough, and it would not in any way impoverish us to dispense with the other nine-tenths.

The issues I have presented here may seem like small details, but now and then we should also consider the small things in life—which have great significance and effect. Then we discover how differently we need to grasp hold of life in order to lead purposeful, healthy lives. It is not always right to send someone to the chemists for medicine when he's ill. Instead we should organize our lives in a way that renders us less susceptible to illness or alleviates its impact. Disorders will impinge on us less severely if we strengthen the ego's influence on the astral body, the astral body's influence on the etheric and the etheric on the physical. Fundamental anthroposophical insights can provide the foundations for self-education and the education of children.

Notes

The text is a record of a lecture Rudolf Steiner gave to members of the Anthroposophical Society in Munich on 11 January 1912.

1. Anthroposophy was the name Steiner gave to his wide-ranging Christ-centred philosophy and practice. Literally it means 'wisdom of the human being'.

2. In Steiner's view we possess, apart from our mineralized physical body, an etheric or life body which we share with the plant kingdom, and an astral or soul body which we have in common with animals. The etheric body is chiefly associated with rhythms, circulation and habitual ways of doing things, while the astral body is the seat of passions, emotions and soul. The fourth and eternal aspect of our being is the 'I' or ego, which continues to exist after death

and subsequently seeks reincarnation in a new body.

3. Two lectures given on 8 and 10 January 1912: 'How to Disprove Theosophy'; and 'How to Prove Theosophy'. (Neither were fully transcribed, and therefore do not appear in Steiner's Collected Works.)

Further Reading

Rudolf Steiner's fundamental books:

Knowledge of the Higher Worlds
also published as: *How to Know Higher Worlds*

Occult Science
also published as: *An Outline of Esoteric Science*

Theosophy

The Philosophy of Freedom
also published as: *Intuitive Thinking as a
Spiritual Path*

Some relevant volumes of Rudolf Steiner's lectures:

Transforming the Soul, Vols. 1 & 2
The Meaning of Life
Self Transformation
The Effects of Esoteric Development
Founding a Science of the Spirit
Rosicrucian Wisdom

For all titles contact Rudolf Steiner Press (UK) or
SteinerBooks (USA):
www.rudolfsteinerpress.com www.steinerbooks.org

Publisher's Note on
Rudolf Steiner's Lectures

The lecture contained in this volume has been translated from the German, which is based on stenographic and other recorded texts that were in most cases never seen or revised by the lecturer. Hence, due to human errors in hearing and transcription, they may contain mistakes and faulty passages. Every effort has been made to ensure that this is not the case. Some of Steiner's lectures were given to audiences more familiar with anthroposophy; these are the so-called 'private' or 'members' lectures. Other lectures, like the written works, were intended for the general public. The difference between these, as Rudolf Steiner indicates in his *Autobiography*, is twofold. On the one hand, the members' lectures take for granted a background in and commitment to anthroposophy; in the public lectures this was not the case. At the same time, the members' lectures address the concerns and dilemmas of the members, while the public work speaks directly out of Steiner's own understanding of universal needs. Nevertheless, as Rudolf Steiner stresses: 'Nothing was ever said that was not solely the result of my direct experience of the growing content of anthroposophy. There was never any question of concessions to the prejudices and preferences of the members. Whoever reads these privately printed lectures can take them to represent anthroposophy in the fullest sense. Thus it was possible without hesitation—when the complaints in this direction became too persistent—to depart from the custom of circulating this material "For members only". But it must be borne in mind that faulty passages do occur in these reports not revised by myself.' Earlier in the same chapter, he states: 'Had I been able to correct them [*the private lectures*], the restriction *for members only* would have been unnecessary from the beginning.'